Ball Lightning and the energy production

TORCHIGIN

CONTENTS

Introduction

One can found by studying various publications in Internet, accessible by keyword «ball lightning» that the term «Low Energy Nuclear Reactions" (LENR) arises in the same publications where the term "ball lightning" is used. Moreover the International conferences devoted to the ball lightning is called "Ball Lightning and «Low Energy Nuclear Reactions". Undoubtedly, the well-known phenomenon of the natural radioactivity is LENR where a nucleus of the radioactive element ceases abruptly its existence. This phenomenon is accompanied by a release of the energy. This energy can be used in practical applications. For example Plutonium-238 has a half-life of 87.7 years, reasonable power density of 0.54 watts per gram and is used as a power supplier for satellites.

However, natural radioactive materials with relatively small half-life are absent on the Earth because they are long gone. We can imagine attempts to decrease the life time of elements, life time of which is great enough and which exist on the Earth. One of these attempts was successful. Nuclear plants produce a noticeable part of the energy for mankind. However, these plants are dangerous and should be cumbersome.

On the other side, successful attempts to decrease the life time by means of great pressure, temperature, powerful electric discharges are known. These attempts are accompanied by arising small luminous objects that are considered as miniature ball lightnings [Levis]

A natural assumption arises that physical conditions within Ball Lightning are favorable for decreasing life-time. However, at present, a generally accepted notion about physical conditions within Ball Lightning is absent. Therefore, it is not clear that physical conditions are required.

In 2002 we put forward a hypothesis that no plasma is responsible for the Ball Lightning existence. Ball Lightning is a pure optical phenomenon. The Ball Lightning can be imagined as the soap bubble where the soap film is replaced by the film of strongly compressed air. The conventional white light is circulating in the film in all possible directions. The film shows itself as a planar wave guide the curvature of which is different from zero. The wave guide prevents the radiation of the light in free space. In turn, the light compresses the air due to the electrostriction pressure. This combination is closer to the light rather than to the lightning. We cut the tail in the world lightning and will call this combination by Ball Light.

The energy of the light is essentially greater than that of the compressed air. In this case the behavior of the Ball Light is determined by the forces connected with the light rather than by the conventional forces connected with material particles. Said forces were considered in numerous hypotheses but all attempts to explain the mysterious behavior of the Ball Lightning failed.

On the contrary, we have succeeded to explain all features of the Ball Lightning behavior on assumption that the forces between the light and matter play a decisive role. Our theory is mentioned in Wikipedia. The following intriguing puzzles of the Ball Lightning behavior are explained in a natural way.

Overcoming Gravity.

Uniform horizontal movement.

Explanation bouncing.

Bypassing obstacles.

Why directions of the wind and a motion of the ball lightning can be different.

Why ball lightning seems cold.

Explanation of circles inside perimeter.

Explanation of the ball lightning motion in a room near a floor rather than near ceiling.

Explanation how the ball lightning finds out splits, holes, and chimneys to penetrate through them.

Explanation of penetration in rooms through small splits and holes.

How the ball lightning enters the room through the window panes.

Behavior of the ball lightning near metal objects.

Why the ball lightning whistles and causes radio interference.

Why the ball lightning of large diameter takes the form of a flying saucer.

Why ball lightnings may have different colors.

Features of the disappearance of ball lightning.

How the ball lightning is catching up a flying aircraft.

At present there is an understanding that Ball Light presents a wide circle of objects of various sizes from a fraction of millimeters till tens meters, with various lifetime from microseconds till tens seconds, with various stored energy from a fraction of Joule till mega Joule. Besides, Ball Light shell can consist of not only compressed air but also various other gases.

In accordance with the theory of the light propagating along a closed trajectory, there are inevitable radiating losses connected with an existence of a tunnel between circulating light and free space. This entails a gradual decrease of the energy stored in the Ball Light. When the energy becomes smaller a certain threshold, the Ball Light becomes instable and disappears abruptly. The light radiates in all sides of free space at the light speed. The air compressed in the spherical layer begins to expand at the sound speed. As a result, the sound like a pistol shot is heard often.

An attempt to extrapolate a notion of ball light for nuclear processes is undertaken. Indeed, there is a natural radioactive decay at which nuclei decays abruptly in the same way as ball lights do. An existence of ball lights is explained by wave phenomena. In accordance with quantum mechanics, an existence of nuclear objects is explained by wave phenomena too. From similarity of nuclei and ball lights disappearance follows that because of inevitable radiation losses inherent to waves of whispering gallery type the energy stored in a nucleus should gradually decrease in time.

As is known, taking into consideration oscillators has allowed Planck, Einstein, Debye and other physicists to develop an absolutely new approach to an explanation of many physical phenomena. Since a classical oscillator was imagined as a mechanical oscillatory system, the further research in this direction have led to the appearance of quantum mechanics although it deals with waves in a form of wave functions. Studying of BL nature has allowed to introduce into consideration other types of oscillators, in particular, oscillators where whispering gallery light waves take part (WGW oscillators). Lifetime of such wave is finite because of inevitable radiating losses inherited to waves of such type.

The further comparison between the WGW oscillators and Ball Light has led to consideration of the self-confined waves of whispering gallery type. In modern terms, such formations are optical spherical spatial solitons (SSS). Ball Light represents the resonator for a light wave of whispering gallery type formed by this wave in a nonlinear optical medium. Unlike usual optical resonators for waves of whispering gallery type [Spillane 2002] in which the light wave of any amplitude can circulate, Ball Light can exist only provided that the amplitude of a circulating wave surpasses some threshold. When the amplitude falls below this threshold because of inevitable radiating losses, Ball Light becomes instable and disappears in the same way, as Ball Lightning does. It is reasonable to assume that whispering gallery waves can exist in quantum mechanics for its wave functions. In this case the energy stored in the nucleus decreases gradually in time.

We will show that this does not contradict to the generally accepted fact that the nucleus energy in unchanged in time. The gradual decrease of the total energy of a system consisting of many identical nuclei manifests itself in abrupt decrease of number nuclei in the system. Since nuclei with smallest energy disappear from the system, the average energy of remained nuclei can be constant in time. Features of interaction of a system of nonlinear identical oscillators are considered. Extrapolation of obtained results on a system of identical nuclei enables to conclude that quickly prepared long-living gas of densely packed molecules is favorable for an increase of the speed of radioactive decay. Numerous experiments confirmed this conclusion are considered.

The same occurs with nuclei of chemical elements. They sharply cease their existence with breaking up and forming other nuclei. This phenomenon has been discovered in the beginning of 20 century and is called as natural radioactive decay. Since this phenomenon reminds existence and disappearance of BL, it is interesting to investigate this similarity in more details. It is especially interesting, as BL and a nucleus are presented by waves. Similarity in the nature of tunnels for light waves in optics and for wave functions in quantum mechanics is so great, that optical analogies are often used for an explanation of tunnel effects in nuclear physics [Vihman 1967]. Therefore, a wave function of a nucleus can be a whispering gallery type too. Certainly, this wave function also satisfies to a wave equation. In this case, similarity becomes full, and all conclusions obtained for self-confined waves of whispering gallery type [Torchigin 2003 -2005] which are a basis of BL theory, can be applied to wave functions too.

A hierarchy of various forms of spherical space solitons (SSS) is presented in figure 1. Till now, we considered the left part of figure where SSS is an abstract notion or theoretical model of BL. The right part presents a particular case of SSS where a wave function is presented by self-confined whispering gallery waves. Nuclei of various chemical elements are their real representatives in the nature.

It is not so hard to convince that the mass of a box in a form of rectangular parallelepiped with mirror inner walls of 100% reflectivity increases by E/c^2 if the box confines any light radiation of energy E. Thus, the mass appears for any confined light radiation, in particular, for self-confined light radiation too. Then one can suppose that any nucleus consists of a set of various SSSs rather than a set of various elementary particles. In this case, the spin of a particle is explained naturally by circulating wave. The charge of a particle appears because of nonlinearity of space. Development of this approach is a task for physicists-theorists. We will try to analyze only the following consequence of this approach Like Ball Light where the intensity of light waves of whispering gallery type gradually decreases in time because of inevitable radiating losses inherent to whispering gallery waves, we need to accept that wave function of SSS decreases gradually in time too. Moreover, we should accept that the square of the module of a wave function characterizes the density of energy, rather than the density of probability as it is usually considered.

Seemingly, these assumptions contradict to the experimental facts according to which the energy of any nucleus is constant in time. Besides, as follows from these assumptions, all nuclei should be stable during all their life, and then they should break up simultaneously when their energy becomes below a certain threshold. It has appeared that these fears are deprived bases. Really, considering nuclei as specific spherical spatial solitons, we should agree that nuclei interact one with another and they exchange by their energy. From here follows, that energies of nuclei are distributed in some narrow interval. When the energy of some nucleus becomes below a certain threshold, it breaks up and disappears from the set of identical interacting nuclei. Disappearance of the nucleus which energy is smaller than the average energy in the set entails an increase in the average energy of the remained nuclei. This shift of the average energy is compensated by a gradual continuous and monotonous reduction of energies in time of all remained nuclei because of radiating losses. As a result, the average energy of nuclei remains constant. External characteristics of radioactive decay completely coincide with experimentally observable ones.

This conclusion is valid in the case where a system of nuclei is in a steady-state. If somehow the steady state is violated, at this time the speed of the radioactive decay can be changed.

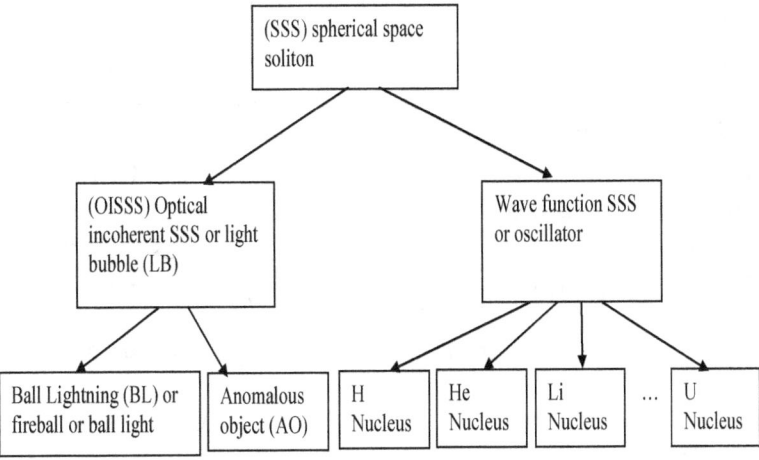

Figure 1. Hierarchy of various types of spherical space solitons and their designations.

Interaction of a Set of Identical Oscillators in a Form of the Self-confined Wave Function

Such oscillators are characterized by a feature that the energy stored in an oscillator decreases gradually in time because of radiating losses. As a result, all oscillators are in the common field produced by them. As is known, radiating losses of an optical oscillator where a light wave of whispering gallery type is circulating are defined by parameter $N = 2\pi r_0/\lambda$, where r_0 is radius of sphere, λ is wavelength of light wave. As shown in [Oraevski 2002], the quality factor determined by radiating losses for a glass ball with $N = 2000$, is equal $Q = 10^{400}$. Energy of oscillations in the resonator decreases as follows

$$E = E_0\exp(-2\omega t/Q) = E_0\exp(-\gamma t), \tag{1}$$

where $\gamma = 2\omega/Q$. Assuming, that for a light wave $\omega = 10^{15}$ c^{-1} and lifetime of light is defined only radiating losses, we obtain unimaginably large value equaled to 10^{378} years.

11

Consider now interaction between a set of chaotically moving identical nonlinear oscillators in which the stored energy gradually decreases in time. Similarly, to molecules of gas in a closed vessel, oscillators can casually collide one with other. Thus everyone oscillator can either acquire or lose any energy at collision. Finally, a normal distribution of energies of oscillators comes (figure2) at which a probability p of an oscillator to have energy in a range from E to $E + \delta E$ is equal to $p(E)\delta E$, where

$$p(E) = \sigma^{-1}\pi^{-1/2}\exp[-(E - E_0)^2/\sigma^2], \qquad (2)$$

$\sigma = F(k)$, $F(k)$ is some increasing function.

As follows from (2), $p(E_{th}) > 0$, where E_{th} is the threshold at which oscillator should disappear. Since a number of nonlinear oscillators in the system decreases, the distribution (2) is pseudo steady-state. Disappearance of an oscillator with minimal energy E_{th} is accompanied by an increase in average energy of remaining oscillators $<E>$ by $(E_0 - E_{th})/N$, where $N \gg 1$ is the number of oscillators in the system. Indeed, the average energy of oscillators can be presented as follows:

$$\langle E \rangle = N^{-1}\sum_{i=1}^{N} E_i = N^{-1}\sum_{i=1}^{N}(E_0 + \Delta E_i) = E_0 + N^{-1}\sum_{i=1}^{N}\Delta E_i \qquad (3)$$

where E_i is an energy of i-th oscillator, $\Delta E_i = E_i - E_0$ and

$$\sum_{i=1}^{N}\Delta E_i = 0$$

Assume that an oscillator with number N disappears. In this case its energy is equal to E_{th}, and the term in (3) for which $\Delta E_N = E_{th} - E_0 < 0$ disappears too.

Then
$$\sum_{i=1}^{N-1}\Delta E_i = (E_0 - E_{th}) > 0$$

and

$$\langle E \rangle = E_0 + (E_0 - E_{th})(N-1)^{-1}. \tag{4}$$

If the number of disappearance per second is λN, then in accordance with (4) the average energy increases by $\lambda(E_0 - E_{th})$. This increase is compensated by a decrease in total energy because of inevitable radiating losses in each oscillator in accordance with the following expression

$$dE/dt = -\gamma E(t) \tag{5}$$

The decrease in accompanied by exchanges of portions of energy at collisions of oscillators. Such exchange promotes that distribution of energy between oscillators tends to normal one. This tendency is violated by disappearance oscillators, which energy is smaller than threshold E_{th}. Thus, the gradual decrease in energy in everyone oscillator is transformed to sequence discrete decreases of the system energy due to disappearance oscillators. Speed of the constant decrease in the total energy is defined (5) and is agreed with the speed of decreasing number of oscillators that is determined as follows

$$dN/dt = -\lambda N(t), \tag{6}$$

where N is total number of oscillators in the system, λ is a probability of disappearance of oscillators per one second. Since the total energy in the system is proportional to the number oscillators in it, then $dN/N = dE/E$, and from (5), (6) we have

$$\lambda = \gamma. \tag{7}$$

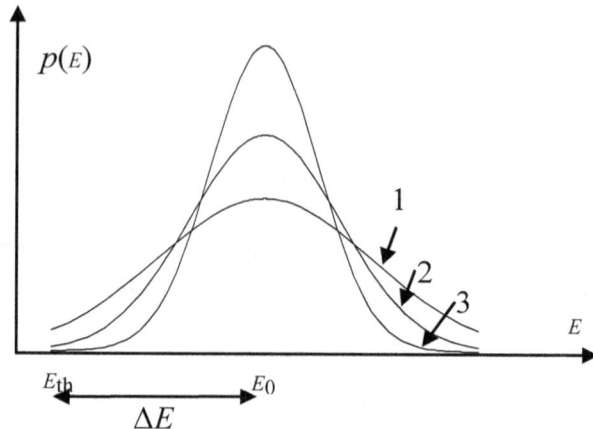

Figure 2. Dependence of density of probability p of appearance of oscillators on their energy E.

Note that this relation depends on neither internal parameters of oscillators, nor on the parameters describing their collisions, such as strength of interaction characterized by dimensionless coupling index k, duration of collision τ_R, frequency of collisions. This conclusion is valid for any system in steady state when average speed of gradual decrease in the total energy is equal to average speed of decrease because of disappearances of oscillators. Let show that this steady state is stable. Let the curve 1 in figure 2 represents normal distribution of the density of probability for oscillator to have energy E. The area under this curve is equal 1. The curve has a maximum at $E = E_0$, and its width depends on the coupling index between oscillators at their collision. If energy of the some oscillator becomes equal E_{th}, oscillator disappears. The smaller difference between E_0 and E_{th}, the greater is probability of its disappearance.

Suppose that maximum of curve 1 takes place at $E = E_1$ where $E_1 < E_0$, that is the curve 1 is shifted to the left. In this case, as follows from figure 2, the speed of disappearance of oscillators raises as compared with the speed at steady state when $E = E_0$. As has been shown, a disappearance of each oscillator is accompanied by an increase in average energy remained oscillators by $\Delta E/N$, where $\Delta E = E_1 - E_{th}$. The greater the speed of disappearances is the greater speed of an increase in average energy. As a result, E_1

increases. This leads to shift of curve 1 to the right, and the speed of disappearance oscillators with energy E_{th} decreases. Such process proceeds until a steady state will be achieved and condition (7) becomes valid. The case when $E_1 > E_0$ can be considered similarly.

Ought to note, that this conclusion is valid for any form of a curve 1. For example, the same reasoning could be applied for curves 2 and 3. It means that the conclusion about validity of condition (7) does not depend on the coupling index. Notice, that number of oscillators which disappear when their energy becomes equal E_{th}, does not depend not only on probability $p(E_{th})$, but also on frequency of collisions. Probability $p(E_0)$ is comparable with $p(E_{th})$ in figure 2 for the sake of illustrative reasons only. Actually $p(E_0)$ is greater than $p(E_{th})$ by many orders of magnitude.

Under assumption that energy of an isolated oscillator is unchanged in time we receive $\gamma = 0$, and, therefore, from (7) $\lambda = 0$. In this case, speed of disappearance of oscillators decreases in time and tends to zero at approach to steady state. This contradicts to experimental data.

Notice that the presented considerations are not valid for transient processes in the system. Consider several examples for the sake of illustration. Assume, that the coupling index becomes equal to zero at $t = 0$. In this case, interaction between oscillators ceases and their energies tend to E_{th} independently. The total energy of the system gradually decreases and maximum of curve 1 in Figure 2 moves in a direction to E_{th}. In this case, the probability of disappearance of oscillators raises with time. Energy oscillators which will disappear at time instant t, is equal $E = E_{th}\exp(\gamma t)$. Taking into account (2), the probability of disappearance of oscillators can be presented as follows:

$$p(t) \sim \exp\left\{-\frac{[E_{th}\exp(\gamma t) - E_0]^2}{\sigma^2}\right\}$$

Curve 1 in figure 3 shows dependence dN/dt on t in steady state when $\gamma = \lambda$, curve 2 shows the same dependence when the coupling index becomes equal to zero at $t = 0$. It is supposed, that $\sigma/E_{th} = 0.05$ and $E_{th}/E_0 = 0.8$. As is seen from figure 3, at $t = 0$, dN/dt for curve 2 is much smaller, than that for curve 1. However at $t \approx$ $0.3t_{0.5}dN/dt$ for curve 2 surpasses dN/dt for curve 1 approximately by 30 times, where $t_{0.5}$ is the time period in which number of oscillators decreases by two times. Dependence dN/dt on t at σ/E_{th} = 0.1 and E_{th}/E_0 = 0.6 is presented by curve 3 in figure3. In this case, maximum of disappearance of oscillators comes later at $t \approx$ $0.75\ t_{0.5}$.

Thus, if the curves similar to dependences 2 and 3 could be obtained experimentally, σ and E_{th}/E_0 could be calculated, and average value of coupling index k could be estimated.

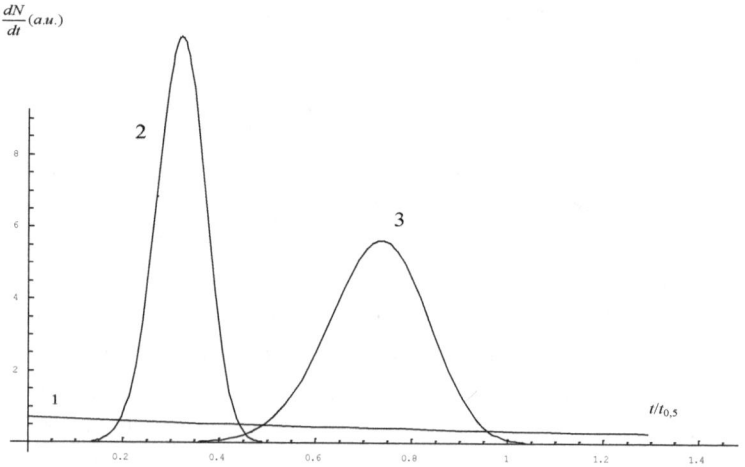

Figure 3. Dependence of radioactive decay on time. 1 – natural decay; 2 – after disappearance of week interaction between oscillators; 3 – after disappearance of strong interaction between oscillators.

The Experimental Data about a Change of Speed of Radioactive Decay with a Change of External Conditions

According to existing representations "λ is one of the major characteristics of atom nucleus: λ does not depend on physical and chemical conditions, such as temperature, pressure, concentration, a chemical compound, from age of a radioactive nucleus" [Encyclopedia of physics 1993]. In our designations, it concerns to a constant γ, which is determined by internal properties of a nucleus and cannot be changed by external forces. In the encyclopedia, it concerns to a constant λ that can be determined experimentally. According to (7) $\lambda = \gamma$ at any steady state. However, these constants can differ during transient processes.

There are enough both old and new works as theoretical so experimental character that point out at an opportunity of changing radioactive decay speed. For example, recently it has been shown, that the greatest stability in isobar series, i.e. among elements with identical nuclear weight, has an atom with minimal energy. Not only very energy of nucleus is taken into account but also the addition in a form of energy of electron environment of the nucleus. This energy is equal to 13.6 eV for hydrogen atom and to several 1000 eVs for atoms with $Z > 20$, where Z is number of protons in an atom. This addition is smaller by 3-4 orders of magnitude than the energy of a nucleus equal approximately $931.5*A$ MeV, where A is atom weight of a nucleus.

Modern accuracy of measurement of atom weights is equal about 1 000 eV. Thus, now energy of atom can be measured in view of energy of an electronic environment. The analysis of accessible experimental data [Audi 1995] has shown that an atom is stable only at a minimum of its energy. Such conditions as "the minimum of weight of a nucleus" or "a maximum of energy of connection" appear wrong [Urutskoev 2004].

This conclusion can be explained in a natural way on the basis of presented approach. Really, a continuous slow decrease in the energy stored in an atom results in a passage of the atom in the new steady state with smaller energy. Such condition is available for all atoms in isobar series, except for atom with minimal energy. For this atom, decrease in the energy should be immeasurably greater that it could pass in the steady state related with another isobar series. Time required for a decrease in the energy in this case should be immeasurably greater. Differently, time of half-decay of such atom should be immeasurably greater, that is it should be practically stable.

There are several important consequences from presented consideration. First, an atom and its electronic environment represent a single whole entity, and it is necessary to consider their general energy. Secondly, difference $E_0 - E_{th}$ is rather small as compared with E_0. In the third, full ionization of atom reduces this difference considerably, as energy of ionization is comparable with the difference between energies of atoms in common isobar series. As the consequence, full ionization of atom should change its half-life period noticeably. Experiments [Jung 1992], [Jelepov 1956] confirm this conclusion. It is shown, that the half-life period completely ionized atom ^{187}Re decreases by in 10^9 times as compared with a neutral atom (the half-life period decreases from $4,3\ 10^{10}$ years to 33 years).

Influence of an electric field of atom on probability of beta decay is considered in details in surveys [Bosh 1996], [Jelepov 1972] where experimental data are presented also. Influence of changes of an electronic environment of atom on beta decay of a nucleus tritium is considered in detail in works [Aculov 2003], [Mamitin 2004] where convincing experimental data are presented also.

It is shown that radiation of uranium after electrolysis increased by 2 times as compared with initial material U_3O_8. As concentration of uranium after electrolysis has appeared at 30 % above, than in the initial material, the normalized emission of α-particles in uranium after electrolysis must became only at 30 % greater than in an initial material [Goddard 2000].

The presented approach, at which the nucleus is considered as spherical self-confined soliton in which the stored energy constantly decreases because of radiating losses, enables to connect a natural radio-activity with gradual decreasing energy of a nucleus. Randomness of natural radioactive decay can be explained not some unknown processes within a nucleus but random processes outside a nucleus provided the stored energy in a nucleus gradually decreases. On assumption that energy of a nucleus is constant, speed of radioactive decay should gradually decrease at the accepted approach. That fact that external conditions can influence at a speed of radioactive decay confirms the right on existence of the presented approach.

Theoretical Preconditions for Increasing Speed of Natural Radioactive Decay

A natural question arises. Whether a speed of radioactive decay can be changed in such a degree that energy that is exerted at any nuclear conversion can be used in alternative sources of energy? As has been shown above, the inner energy within a nucleus decreases gradually in time as well as changes abruptly at collision of nuclei. When the inner energy decreases down to the threshold at which the nucleus becomes instable, the nucleus breaks up and some excess energy liberates from the nuclei. Unfortunately, the intensity of this process is extremely small for all of natural chemical elements. By the way, such process is used in Plutonium power suppliers located on satellites. Their power is about 3 kW and duration of operating is about 80 years. But they are very expensive devices because very expensive substance is used as a fuel. Usual natural matter widely spread in nature is desirable to use as a fuel.

The simplest way to increase the speed of a radioactive decay is to increase coupling index k that characterizes strength of interaction. It turns out that it is insufficient. Unlike molecules of gas which are considered as elastic balls at their interaction at collisions and their energy is proportional to the square of their velocity, interaction of oscillators is perfectly different. Firstly, the energy of oscillator is not connected with its velocity. In this case motionless adjacent oscillators can interact one with another and duration of their interaction can be as great as is wished. Secondly, an oscillator is excellent accumulator of energy if the speed of transmission of energy into the oscillator is greater essentially than the speed of a decrease of energy due to radiating loses. Reality shows that this condition is held with great because oscillators exist in many billions years. Thirdly, transmission of energy between oscillators depends on phase relations between oscillations within them. Transmission of energy is absent completely at certain phase relations.

Consider features of interaction of a system of oscillators to clarify a possibility of using these features to accelerate their disappearance. Initially the simplest case of interaction of two coupled oscillators is considered.

Interaction of Two Interconnected Oscillators

A theory of interconnected oscillators is well developed and is used in many absolutely different applications. We present its results used in the further consideration. In the elementary case the following system linear differential equations describes change of complex amplitudes a_1 and a_2 in identical oscillators 1 and 2, respectively, with identical eigen frequencies ω [17]:

$$da_1/dt = j\omega a_1 + jk\omega a_2$$
$$da_2/dt = j\omega a_2 + jk\omega a_1. \tag{8}$$

Here dimensionless coupling index $k = j\kappa/\omega$, where κ is the coupling index used in [17]. The system (8) has two eigen frequencies

$$\omega_1 = (1 - k)\omega \tag{9}$$

and

$$\omega_2 = (1 + k)\omega, \tag{10}$$

which correspond symmetrical $\{a_1 = \exp(j\omega_1 t), a_2 = \exp(j\omega_1 t)\}$ and anti symmetrical $\{a_1 = \exp(j\omega_2 t), a_2 = -\exp(j\omega_2 t)\}$ eigen solutions. Any linear combination of these eigen solutions is also a solution of the system (8). Any solution describes beatings which amplitude and phase depend on initial conditions at $t = 0$.

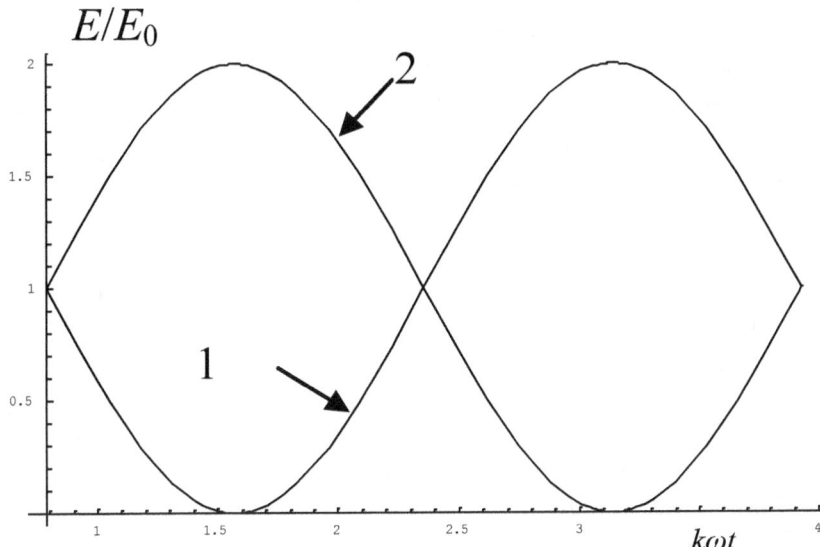

Figure 4. Dependences of energies of two interconnected oscillators on time at optimal phase relations: Curves 1 and 2 show dependencies for the first and second oscillators, respectively.

For example, if $a_1(0) = 1$, $a_2(0) = 0$, then $a_1(t) = \cos(\Omega t) \exp(j\omega t)$, $a_2(t) = \sin(\Omega t) \exp(j\omega t)$, where

$$\Omega = k\omega \qquad (11)$$

is a frequency of beatings that does not depend on the initial conditions. Since the energy stored in an oscillator is proportional to a square of amplitude of oscillations, then

$$E_1(t) \sim \cos^2(\Omega t), \ E_2 \sim \sin^2(\Omega t), \qquad (12)$$

where $E_1(t)$, $E_2(t)$ are energies stored in oscillators 1 and 2, respectively. It easy to see that $E_1(t) + E_2(t) =$ const. Dependences of energies of two interconnected oscillators on time at optimal phase relations are shown in figure 4.

A transfer of energy between two identical nuclei depends on phase relations between oscillations in them. A transfer of energy is absent only in the eigen solutions in which phases are identical in the symmetric own solutions or differ by π; for antisymmetric one. Speed of transfer of energy is maximal, if amplitudes of oscillations are identical, and their phases differ by $\pi/2$. The first condition is valid for nuclei.

The second condition can appear valid accidentally. In general, transfer of energy takes place at any phase difference φ. However the amplitude of beatings can change from zero (when the difference of phases is equal 0 or π) up to maximal. Transfer of energy takes place at any coupling index k but the speed of transfer is proportional to k. It is possible to conclude, that appreciable interaction between oscillators is possible at any distance between them provided that duration of interaction τ_b is comparable with the beating period $2\pi/\Omega$.

$$\tau_b \cong 2\pi/\Omega = 2\pi/(k\omega) = \tau_n/k. \tag{13}$$

where $\tau_n = 2\pi/\omega$.

As to coupling index k that it is known reliable that k is extremely small. As shown in [Haus 1984], appreciable interaction between two oscillators with own frequencies ω_a and ω_b, takes place, if the following condition $(\omega_a - \omega_b)/\omega_a < k$ is valid. In this case the difference between own frequencies of any two unequal nuclei is so great, that this condition is not valid. Thus, a noticeable interaction can be only between identical nuclei.

It is necessary to take into account that the nuclei considered as oscillators are a typical "nonlinear oscillating system". It means that properties of nuclei depend on amplitude of oscillations. In our example energy of oscillations increases in one nucleus by 12 % and decreases in other nucleus in time $0.01\tau_b$. The difference in amplitudes can become so great, that the stationary condition of nuclei occur violated and the system from two interconnected nuclei can pass in a new steady state characterized by a new local minimum of the total energy that is smaller than previous minimum was. Thus, superfluous energy is liberated. For example, there can be a synthesis of two nuclei of deuterium. On the contrary, for heavy nuclei, for example, uranium, there can be a nuclear reaction of division. In any case, own frequencies of oscillators after liberation of the excess energy become various and their interaction stops. Thus, any noticeable changes in action R can be only between identical nuclei.

Ought to note that instable states of a nucleus uses in the nuclear physics for a long time for an explanation of that fact, that a slow neutron can split a nucleus ^{235}U better, than a fast neutron. Unlike a fast neutron, a slow neutron can be absorbed by nucleus; it becomes instable and disintegrated as a result of this instability. We are going to show that instable states can appear not only under action of slow neutrons, but also as a result of long interaction of two identical nuclei.

Interaction of a Set of Oscillators

It is simply enough to imagine a picture of interaction of two nuclei located near each another for a long time. But how such picture can be realized? As is seen from (13), the degree of interaction R at the maximal speed of transfer of energy is determined by the expression:

$$R = \Delta E/E_0 = 2\Omega\tau = 2\omega k\tau, \tag{14}$$

where $\Delta E/E_0 \ll 1$ is a relative change of the energy in time τ. We have from (14) that R is maximal when product of $k\tau$ is as much as possible at optimum phase relations. The coupling index k can be increased by decreasing a distance r between oscillators. The most radical way to decrease r is to increase density of interacting oscillators.

Seemingly, liquids or solids are the most suitable candidates for realization of great interaction between oscillators because their nuclei are located to each other closer than in gases. However, it appears that in these conditions a majority of interconnected oscillators is in a steady state and the difference of phases of oscillations between adjacent interacting oscillators is equal to zero. In this case, there is no interaction between oscillators. Interaction of a set of mutually interconnected oscillators is well enough studied in radio engineering as a set of mutually connected oscillators in the form of LC circuits is used in high-quality radio receivers. Nuclei in liquids or solids considered as interconnected oscillators form a specific three-dimensional transmission line in which any deviation from a stationary condition in any oscillator at once begins to propagate in all directions through a chain of interconnected adjacent oscillators.

The more coupling index between oscillators the greater the speed of propagation of the deviations. In other words, oscillators are synchronous among themselves. Certainly, there are some small deviations from steady state because of thermal motions of atoms, but these deviations cannot lead to a sharp increase in amplitude of some oscillators.

Like a random motion of gas molecules cannot entail a sharp increase in gas density, small random phase shifts cannot entail significant increase in amplitudes of oscillations. Any increase in amplitude of oscillations entails immediate scattering. Thus, liquids or solids do not permit to accumulate results of interactions because phase relations between oscillators are far from required ones.

Absolutely other situation takes place in a set of moving oscillators presented by atoms of gas at normal conditions. In this case time of collision oscillators is much smaller than time of free movement between two consecutive collisions. Each collision is accompanied by occurrence of a system consisting of two interconnected oscillators. In such system its own frequency can change in a range $(1 - k)\omega < \omega < (1 + k)\omega$ and depends on phase relation between oscillations in the oscillators.

The change in own frequency leads to change of phases of oscillators as compared with a phase of an isolated oscillator with own frequency ω. Change of phases of oscillators can be both positive and negative depending on initial phases between interacting oscillators. The total phase shift appeared as a result of one collision depends on force (k) and time of interaction. The smaller distance between interacting nuclei, the greater phase shift at one collision. Thus, unlike system motionless interacting oscillators where certain phase relations between adjacent oscillators take place, the steady state of a system of chaotically moving and colliding oscillators is characterized by random phases of each oscillator.

It is easy to be convinced, that if phase relations at each collision are random, the probability that favorable collisions considerably prevail above unfavorable ones is negligible small. This conclusion does depend on neither pressure nor temperatures of gas. Because of this, it is useless to try to increase result of interaction by means of increase these parameters. Thus, neither solids nor liquids nor gases can provide significant change in energy of oscillators. Seemingly, our attempts to use features of oscillators for significant change of their energy are fruitless. However, non steady states have been not analyzed yet.

Effect of Repeated Long Interaction

Assume, that gas is compressed up so, that oscillators of gas are densely packed in such degree, that the volume per one oscillator is equal to volume of the oscillator. In such gas an effect that enables to accumulate significantly result of interaction R appears. Unlike gas at normal conditions where each oscillator collides each following time with a new oscillator and a probability of collision in the near future with a former oscillator is extremely small, the behavior of an oscillator in gas of densely packed oscillators is absolutely different. Each oscillator oscillates in an environment of the same adjacent oscillators that do not allow it to move freely. In this case, two identical adjacent oscillators can interact many times between themselves and accumulate result of interaction R.

Phases of oscillations in homogeneous gas of densely packed oscillators are random; at least, they are random after sharp compression. In this case, the probability that the area where R can be accumulated noticeably is rather great. Really, if oscillator is surrounded by K identical oscillators, the probability that phases of all these oscillators are favorable for transmit of energy to central oscillator is equal to $p = 2^{-K}$. For example, if $K = 6, p = 1.6 \ 10^{-2}$. As the total number of oscillators $N \cong 10^{20}$ cm^{-3}, the number of such areas is rather great.

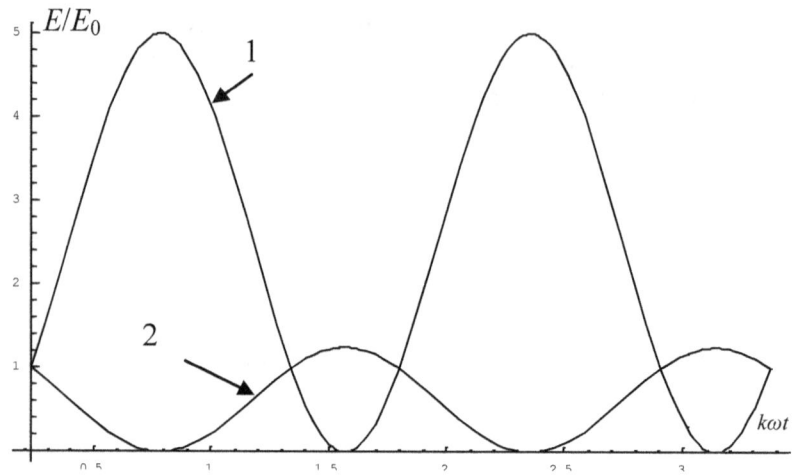

Figure 5. Dependence of the energy in five interacting oscillators on time: 1 – energy of oscillators surrounded by four other oscillators; 2 – energy of each of these oscillators.

Generalizing (8) on five oscillators, one of which is located in the point with coordinates $(x = 0, y = 0)$, and others are located in points with coordinates: $(x = 0, y = 1)$, $(x = 0, y = -1)$, $(x = 1, y = 0)$, $(x = -1, y = 0)$, we receive dependences of energy oscillators on time, shown in figure 5. It is supposed, that energies of all oscillators at $t = 0$ are identical, and the phase of oscillations in the first oscillator lags behind by $\pi/2$ from phases of others oscillators. As follows from figure 5, the maximal energy in the first oscillator increases by 2.5 times, and the period of beatings decreases by 2 times as compared with figure 4. Speed of increase in energy in the first oscillator at $t = 0$ in figure 5 is greater by 8.9 times, than that in figure 4. It means that action of 4 adjacent oscillators with favorable phases is stronger by 8.9 times than action of one oscillator.

Possibly, it is difficult enough to provide optimal conditions for accumulation of energy from K oscillators and they can be realized only at extremely favorable phase relations. For example, if to admit that the probability of extremely favorable phase relations between two adjacent oscillators is equal $p = 0.1$ instead of $p = 0.5$ the probability of extremely favorable phase relations in a system from $K + 1$ oscillators is equal 10^{-K}. Thus, the greater K, the more favorable conditions can be obtained, but a probability of such conditions decreases with growth K.

Usually, when any transient processes in some system are considered, a time constant is introduced which characterizes how quickly the system tends to its steady state. From this reasoning ought to introduce a time constant τ_R, which characterizes the time required to a system to pass from a gas of densely packed oscillators with random phases in the steady state when phases of all oscillators are identical.

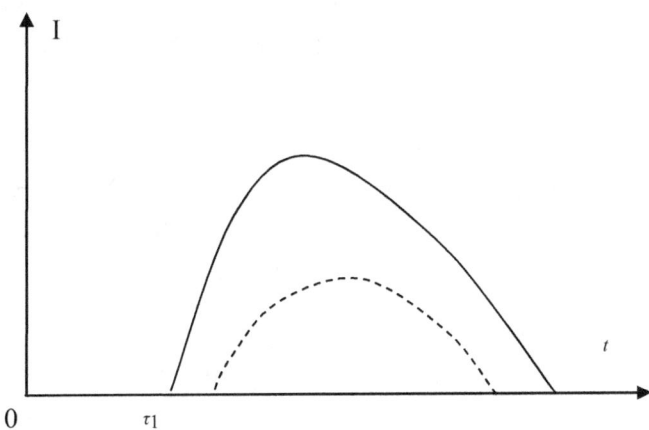

Figure 6. Dependence of the speed of radioactive decay on time.
Solid curve corresponds to instant compression, dotted curve – gradual compression.

However before it is necessary to find some mechanism responsible for dissipation of energy in a non-equilibrium system because energy of the system at steady state should be minimal. Action of this mechanism determines value of the time constant. For example, in gases, this constant differs significantly for different mechanisms. In gases it is necessary only 1-2 collisions between molecules for a forward-forward relaxation, 4-5 collisions for rotary-rotary one and about 10^{20} collisions for oscillating-oscillating one [Luybitov 1998].

In accordance with (9) own frequency of a system of two interconnected oscillators with synchronous oscillations decreases at nearing oscillators. Then in accordance with Manley-Rowe relations energy of such system decreases. It means that oscillators are drawn one to other. As a result, in liquid or solid, consisting from such oscillators, there are forces of compression that leads to appearance of elastic fluctuations with corresponding dissipation of energy. Unfortunately, the physical nature of these forces of an attraction is not known to us. We can remind only that the physical nature of gravitation forces is not known also. Possibly, these forces can have an identical origin as well as dark matter and/or dark energy are connected with them.

As follows from presented theoretical consideration, the following conditions should be provided for noticeable increase in R. First, compression of gas should be so much strong that molecules of gas have appeared densely packed close together. Secondly, they should remain densely packed for a long time. In the third, duration of transient on compression of gas should be no more τ_R. Summarization of all this three conditions enables to claim that a quickly prepared long-living gas of densely the packed molecules is necessary for obtaining areas where a noticeable increase in R is possible

As the maximal coupling index k_{max} between oscillators is small, areas with noticeable increase in R can be obtained if time of interaction between oscillators is greater than a certain bottom threshold τ_{min}. As follows from (14),

$$\tau_{min} = R/(2\omega k_{max}). \tag{15}$$

If duration of interaction is smaller than τ_{min}, appearance of areas with noticeable increase in R is impossible.

The solid curve in figure 6 shows dependence of the number of oscillators I which energy decreases down till E_{th} at the assumption that gas is compressed instantly at $t = 0$. The curve is received on the basis of following qualitative consideration. Time τ_1 is minimal time, which is required to accumulate the action at an assumption that the oscillator occurs at optimum phase relations with other interacting oscillators. As the probability of such situation is small, the number is close to zero. With increase in time of interaction, E_{th} is reached at phase relations which differ from optimal ones a little. The probability of such phase relations is greater and, hence, the number is also greater. At the further increase in time of interaction the number I can start to decrease, because there is an alignment of phases in adjacent oscillators, and the exchange of energy between them ceases.

If compression of gas occurs not instantly, dependence of the number I on time is described by curve shown in figure 6 by dashed line. The following features of this dependence ought to notice. The delay τ_1 after which I becomes different from zero increases because of transient processes which take place during compression of gas. These transients at which phases of all oscillators are leveled, do not allow to receive optimum phase relations at $t > \tau_1$. The maximum of a curve decreases. Ought to underline, that I is always equal to zero at $t < \tau_1$ and, hence, long compression always is required. If speed of transients is greater than speed of compression, I is close to zero as the system is in quasi steady state where the exchange of energy between oscillators practically is absent.

Thus, we can wait a noticeable increase in a speed of radioactive decay in a quickly prepared long living gas of densely packed molecules.

The Analysis of the Physical Conditions in Experiments Accompanied by Nuclear Conversions

Meaning simple theoretical conclusions received above, we shall analyze conditions of successful experiments known to us in which anomalous phenomena were observed. It has appeared that in all experiments quickly prepared long living gas of densely packed molecules took place. Ought to note that the shell of the ball light consisting of strongly compressed air can appear extremely quickly during a fraction of a microsecond. There are some experimental confirmations of this fact [Urutskoev 2002]. It is no wonder because light participates in its formation and makes thousand revolutions in the shell in this time. Thus, physical conditions inside of an AO shell are suitable for increasing radioactive decay. AO shell is, probably, a single object among known ones which provides necessary physical conditions at which time of interaction $t > \tau_1$. Analysis of experimental studies where a mention about nuclear conversions takes place shows that AOs are observed in the great bulk of these studies. There is one group of the studies where nuclear conversions are observed but direct mentions about AOs absent. But a quickly prepared long living gas of densely packed molecules is presented in these studies too. Consider results of some experiments.

At first sight, no such gas existed in classical Pons and Fleishman experiments connected with electrolysis of palladium electrodes in heavy water. Really, it seemed so within 14 years. In 2003, as a result 14-years research the following facts [Storm 2003] have been established. First, areas in which nuclear activity takes place lay on a surface of the cathode, instead of inside of metal as it was supposed earlier. Secondly, these areas exist in dendrites or nano crystals, located on a surface of an electrode, instead of on the very surface. A conclusion has been drawn that the only thing necessary for a nuclear conversion is existence of the small isolated domains of a material. It can be dendrites growing on a surface of the electrode or impregnations in the

30

palladium electrode, or grains of other material on the palladium electrode. Erosive discharges on these inhomogeneities can occur

These conclusions were confirmed in Szpak work [Szpak 2003], where was shown that nuclear conversion is accompanied by occurrence on a surface of electrode of "hot spots" and micro explosions. It was estimated that each micro explosion is accompanied by a nuclear conversion in which from 10^4 up to 10^9 nuclei participate. It is not excluded, that the reason of micro-explosion is disappearance of a miniature ball lightnings have appeared as a result of local erosive discharges. The term "miniature ball lightning" means the same that our term "autonomous object". We shall use already accepted term though the term miniature ball lightning is more often used. Japanese investigator Matsumoto [Matsumoto 1995-2001] repeatedly informed about observation of AOs in conditions of classical Pons and Fleishman experiments

Lewis analyzed surfaces of those cathodes that have been used in successful attempts to carry out nuclear conversion. It turns out that these cathodes, unlike other cathodes, have been undergone to strong erosion [Lewis 2003]. Besides, occurrence of AOs from their surface was observed in a process of nuclear conversion. Similar erosion of electrodes is observed in numerous experiments on AO production by means of erosive gas discharge [Avramenko 1994]. Thus, at present time it is authentically established that nuclear conversion in conditions of classical experiment is accompanied by occurrence AOs and, therefore, there is a quickly prepared long living gas of densely packed molecules.

Such gas presents also in cavitation bubbles produced in liquids by means of an intensive acoustic wave. It is known, that pressure in such bubbles at their compression can reach several thousand atmospheres. As was shown in Kladov experiences carried out in 1998-2001, nuclear conversion took place in such bubbles [Kladov 1998-2001]. Analogous experiences have been carried out by Taleyarkhan group in 2004. Now this group is financed by DARPA.

The conclusion that the gas obtained at explosions accompanied by erosion of a material is favorable for nuclear conversion has been confirmed by Ukrainian scientists who used a powerful pulse of electrons with energy about 1 kJ for super compression of substance [Adamenko 2004].

It would seem, the gas is absent in Correa experiments connected with production of excess energy by means of vacuum discharges. [Carrel 1996]. However, works of other researchers, in particular, Shoulders showed that the vacuum discharge is accompanied by occurrence of so-called exotic vacuum objects and transmutation of elements [Shoulders 2005]. In reality, such objects represent AOs, and their shape where intensive light circulates consists of vapors of metal that are evaporated from the cathode of a vacuum tube. Thus, the gas consists of molecules of metal in this case. The same is valid for Solin experiments with welding of zirconium in vacuum by electronic beam [Solin 2001].

By the way, Sholders studies allow to explain existence of ectons which are avalanches of electrons arising at the vacuum discharge [Mesyats 2000]. An appearance of an avalanche can be explained somehow within a frame of usual representations without attraction of AO but it is impossible to find out reasonable reasons caused a disappearance of an avalanche. As was shown in chapter 2, introduction of AOs into consideration of the phenomena at vacuum discharges enables to explain both occurrence, and disappearance of avalanches, and also the fact of their existence. Introduction of AOs into consideration permits also to explain occurrence of excess energy in Correa experiences because any appearance of AOs is accompanied by appearance of a quickly prepared long living gas of densely packed molecules. The excess energy appears due to acceleration of nuclear decay. Indeed, transmutation of elements has been fixed in Sholders experiments.

R.F. Avramenko has informed about generation of excess energy by means of AOs in a form of so-called great energy plasma formations [Avramenko 1994. In this case, AOs were produced by erosive gas discharge in air at normal atmosphere pressure. Urutskoev has informed about a transmutation of elements at explosions of titanic wires at discharge of the battery of capacitors about 50 kJ stored energy [Urutskoev 2002]. He has marked that the explosions are accompanied by occurrence of "spherical plasma formations". In reality, they are AOs. By the way, the fact of extremely fast occurrence of ball lights has been fixed in these experiments in the first time. It has appeared, that at shooting by high-speed video camera a ball light appears so quickly, that it is absent on one frame, and it has been generated completely on the following frame.

Thus, introduction of AOs into consideration allows finding out some common and explaining seemingly absolutely different experiments. All known experiments on successful realization of nuclear conversions, where either generation of excess energy, or transmutation of elements takes place, are accompanied by an appearance of a quickly prepared long living gas of densely packed molecules.

Some views on order of magnitude constants used above can be obtained from analysis of physical conditions of successful experiments accompanied by nuclear conversions. Since life time of AO is in the interval from 1mks to 1 ms and the lifetime is comparable with the time constant τ_{NC} for passing a system of densely packed oscillators in a steady state, then τ_{NC} is in an interval from 10^{-6} up to 10^{-3} s. The beating period is greater by 1-2 orders of magnitude than τ_{NC} and, hence, and τ_b is in an interval from 10^{-5} up to 10^{-1}s.

According to modern representations of nuclear physics "in a nucleus, considered in a form of a drop [Pik—Pichak 1990], there are oscillations with the period $\tau_n = 10^{-21}$s and amplitude equaled to 0,1-0,2 radius of a nucleus ". Taking into account that $\tau_n \approx 10^{-21}$ s, we obtain from (13) $k = \tau_n/\tau_b \approx 10^{-20}–10^{-16}$. Certainly, these evaluations are only an illustration of how extremely small coupling index can lead to an appreciable result for reasonable time.

Observation of appearing AOs testifies that physical conditions in AOs are favorable for acceleration of nuclear decay. Since the nature of AOs is known, these conditions can be created in laboratory. It is known, that experiments with nuclear conversions are characterized weak reproducibility. Low reproducibility takes place also in experiments on AOs production because a physical nature of AOs was not known for experimenters. Purposeful use of erosive gas discharge allows to eliminate the specified lack and to start purposeful accomplishment of nuclear conversions. In accordance with one of hypotheses, the Ball Lightning was a reason of Chernobyl tragedy [Torchigin 2006], which essentially delayed development of atomic engineering. It is not excluded, that the Ball Lightning will expiate the fault and will play solving positive role in development of absolutely new direction in nuclear energetic which will lead to development of new cheap alternative energy sources. How the life on the earth will be changed is described by American futurologist Arthur Clark [Clarke 1992].

Possible Types of Nuclear Decays

From the presented consideration follows that interaction of only identical nuclei can accelerate a nuclear decay. Besides, the smaller the difference between the energy stored in a nucleus before decay and after decay the easier conditions for realization of such conversion can be fulfilled. What types of nuclear conversions can be carried out by means of accumulation of interaction between adjacent identical nuclei? It is not difficult to find out a majority of possible decays in which the minimal excess energy takes place. In this case the total number of protons and neutrons is kept after conversion.

Similarly to classical reaction of synthesis of deuterium nuclei

$$2\,{}^{2}_{1}D \rightarrow {}^{4}_{2}He + 23{,}8 \text{ MeV},$$

We can write, for example, the following reactions

$$2\,{}^{27}_{13}Al \rightarrow {}^{26}_{12}Mg + {}^{28}_{14}Si + 3{,}315 \text{ MeV},$$

$$2\,{}^{63}_{29}Cu \rightarrow {}^{64}_{30}Zn + {}^{62}_{28}Ni + 1{,}59 \text{ MeV}.$$

The excess energy is determined by the difference in mass defects ΔM between initial and resulting products. In accordance with [Grigoriev 1991] ΔM for considered nuclei are the following:

ΔM for $^{27}_{13}Al$ – 17,194 MeV,

ΔM for $^{26}_{12}Mg$ – 16,212 MeV,

ΔM for $^{28}_{14}Si$ – 21,491 MeV,

ΔM for $^{63}_{29}Cu$ – 65,578 MeV,

ΔM for $^{64}_{30}Zn$ – 66,001 MeV,

ΔM for $^{62}_{28}Ni$ – 66,745 MeV.

Notice, that the left hand side in the record of reactions begins with number 2. It means that identical nuclei can participate in reaction only. The first reaction with deuterium is reaction of synthesis. However, it is impossible to tell the same about the second and third reactions as two nuclei exist before and after reaction. After the analysis ΔM for some heavy nuclei, it is possible to write, for example, the following reaction:

$$2^{206}_{82}Pb \rightarrow ^{206}_{82}Pb + 2^{103}_{41}Nb + 102.23 MeV$$

This is typical reaction of radioactive decay with generation about 100 MeV additional energy. Actually there is a splitting *Pb* nucleus on 2 identical *Nb* nuclei by means of other *Pb* nucleus that is accompanied by generation of superfluous energy. Certainly, splitting can occur and on not identical nuclei. Thus, there can be a synthesis of nuclei, their splitting, and also transmutation of elements, at which two identical nuclei are transformed in various nuclei. Thousands of similar reactions can be imaged. The considered examples are only an illustration. The analysis of possible types of nuclear conversion is a problem of nuclear physics. We would like to note only one obvious conclusion. The smaller life time of a nucleus or excess energy are the easier to carry out nuclear conversion with such nucleus. Indeed, in this case there are either relatively great radiating losses or/and a small difference E_0-E_{th}.

An isotopic conversion is accompanied by small excess energy. What is why a change of a natural isotopic ratio is mentioned often. It is very pictorial experiments of Urutskoev at explosion of a titanic wire that were accompanied by appearance of AOs. Natural isotopic ratio changed after the explosion as follows. A fraction of isotope Ti^{48} decreased from 72 % up to 62 %, percent of isotopes Ti^{46}, Ti^{47}, Ti^{49}, Ti^{50} increased from 8 % up to 10 %, from 6 % up to 8 %, from 10 % up to 12 %, from 6 % up to 8 %, respectively. Unfortunately, the paper with these data disappeared from Internet. Mention about these reactions is in [Vysotskii 2003]. Apparently, there were nuclear conversions of the following type

$$2^{48}_{22}Ti \rightarrow ^{49}_{22}Ti + ^{47}_{22}Ti + 3,485 \ \text{МэВ}$$

or

$$2^{48}_{22}Ti \rightarrow ^{50}_{22}Ti + ^{46}_{22}Ti + 0,420 \ \text{МэВ}$$

In the first case one neutron passes from one nucleus in others and in the second case two neutrons pass.

Probably, similar reactions are used by colonies microbiological cultures in radioactive waste with rather small life time. There is evidence that in such environments transmutation of elements is possible. Besides, the speed of radioactive decay noticeably increases [Urutskoev 2002]. Thus there are neither explosions, nor intensive light, nor any AOs.

"Micro installation" in a form of a bacterium can be imagined which have learned to break a stationary phase relation between adjacent oscillators by sharp relocation of oscillators. As a result, the coupling index between oscillators and their own frequencies change. It causes phase shift of oscillations in these oscillators relative a phase of oscillations in an isolated oscillator. When the phase shift reaches $\pi/2$, the bacterium nears the oscillator with other oscillator having the steady state phase. As a result, the phase shift between these oscillators becomes equal to $\pi/2$. This provides transmission of energy from one oscillator to others. Thus the bacterium accelerates a decrease in energy of nucleus until its energy achieves threshold E_{th} and the nucleus breaks up. Excess energy generated at this process is used by bacterium for ability to live.

As a rule, coupling index between usual nuclei is so small and the difference E_0-E_{th} is so great that the bacterium is not able to provide a necessary decrease in E_0 down to E_{th}. But the situation can be favorable for nuclei with rather small half-life period. There is double usefulness from small half-life period of a nucleus. Firstly, the smaller half-life period of a nucleus the greater the amplitude of wave function outside the nuclei because in accordance with generally accepted notions the square of the wave function outside a nucleus is proportional to the probability of its decay. In this case coupling index between adjacent nuclei is greater than that between nuclei with great half-life period. Secondly, the difference E_0-E_{th} is small enough because the excess energy is small. Radioactive waste with rather small life time contains such nuclei. Bacteria have learned to extract and use excess energy for their life earlier, than the people have. Bacteria have advantage over people because there are no theorists among bacteria who assert that it is impossible.

Certainly, it is very hard work to find out the most suitable new fuel for new alternative sources of energy. On the one hand, it should be a wide spread element with relatively long life time so that it is not dangerous for health. On the other hand, its excess energy at accelerated nuclear decay should be considerable and conditions for production of a quickly prepared long living gas of densely packed molecules should be as simple as possible. Thus, instead of a single nuclear reaction of synthesis of deuterium nuclei which takes place in H-bomb there are a lot of other nuclear reaction which are also accompanied by appearance of excess energy. Possibly, presented above our rough consideration can determine a direction of further investigations. Ought to underline that there is no mystics. Indeed, natural radioactive decay is an objective reality. Possibility of changing the speed of radioactive decay is also objective reality. Appearance of excess energy and transmutation of elements are also objective realities. Everything that is required it is to find out a way of using these realities in practical applications.

Conclusion

Extension of processes and the phenomena occurring in a ball light on nuclei of elements allows to explain the phenomenon of natural radioactive decay. Just as the energy stored in a ball light is gradually decreasing and the ball light becomes instable, energy of a nucleus gradually decreases in time too; the nucleus becomes instable and breaks up. It is shown that if interaction between nuclei is taken into account then such assumption does not contradict to reliable experimental data according to which average energy of a nucleus does not depend on time. The experimental data confirming these conclusions and testifying that external conditions can influence on the speed of a radioactive decay are presented.

An attempt to find the means allowing to increase the speed of radioactive decay has been undertaken. With this purpose, the nucleus has been presented in a form of nonlinear oscillator with a definite life time. An interaction of a set of such identical oscillators has been considered. It is shown, that for a noticeable decrease in energy of the some oscillator it is necessary to randomize initially phases of all oscillators, and then to pack these oscillators as quickly and densely as possible to provide condition that the relative positioning of oscillators would be kept in a relatively long time. The derived conclusions can be used not only for realization of nuclear reactions of decay but also for nuclear reactions at which transmutation of elements occurs. It is shown that such reactions could be carried out in the quickly prepared long-living gas of densely packed molecules. Numerous experimental data supporting this conclusion are presented.

Reference

Aculov Yu. A., Mamirin B. A., Usp. Fiz. Nauk 2003, 173, 1187.

Adamenko S. V., Adamenko A. S., Vysotskii V. I., 2004. Infinite Energy, 9 (54), 23–30.

Audi G.,. Wapstra A.H. Nucl. Phys., 1995 A 595, 409.

Avramenko R. F, Nikolaeva V. I., Poskacheva L. P In book Ball lightning in laboratory. Editor Avramenko R. F. Himiya, Moscow, 1994, pp. 7-56 (in Russian).

Avramenko R. F.Ed. Ball Lightning in a laboratory, (Moscow, Himiya, 1994).

Bosh A. et al. 1996. Phys Rev. Lett. 77, 5190

Carrel, Mike, (1996). In Infinite Energy Magazine Special Selection pp. 62–70.

Clarke A. C., (1992). The coming age of Hydrogen Power. Infinite Energy Magazine Special Selection, pp.8–10.

Encyclopedia of Physics (Mc Graw-Hill, 1993).

Goddard G., Dash O. Trans. American Nuclear Soc. 2000, 83, 301.

Grigoriev I. S. Handbook of physical Quantities, Ed. (Energoatomizdat, Moscow 1991; CRC Press, Boca Raton, 1997)

Haus H.A. Waves and Fields in Optoelectronics (Prentice Hall, New Jersey) 1984.

Jelepov B. S.; Ziryanova L. N. SuslovYu. P. Beta processes: functions for analysis of beta spectrums and electron capture; Nauka: Leningrad, 1972.

Kladov A. In 13-th Radiochemical Conference. 19–24 April, 1998. Marianske Lazne Jachymov Czech Republic. Booklet of Abstracts.

Kladov A. In 21-th International Symposium «Industrial Texicology 2001». Proceedings. 30 May – 1 June 2001, Bratislava, Slovak Republic.

Kladov, A. In 5-th International Conference on Nuclear and Radiochemistry. Pontresina, Switzerland, 3–8 September, 2000, Extended Abstracts vol. 1.

Lewis, E. H., In Tenth International Conference on Cold Fusion, USA, Massachusetts, Cambridge, August, 2003.

Luybitov, Yu. N. In Physical encyclopedia, Prokhorov, A., M.; Ed.; Bolshaya Rosiyskaya Ensiklopediya: Moscow, 1998, Vol. 1, pp 375–379.

Mamirin, B.,A.; Akulov, Yu., A.Usp. Fiz. Nauk; 2004, 174, 791.

Matsumoto T., Fifth International Conference on Cold Fusion. 1995 April 9–13, Monte Carlo, Monako.

Matsumoto, T. Fusion Technology, 1992, 22, 281.

Matsumoto, T., 2001. IEEE International Pulsed Power Conference, 2001, 1, 273–276.

Mesyats, G. A. Ectons in vacuum discharge: discharge, spark, arc; Nauka: Moscow, 2000.

Mesyats, G.A., 1995. Uspehi Physics;1995 165 (6), 601–626.

Oraevskiy, A. N. Quantum electronics; 2002, 32, № 5, 377–400.

Pik-Pichak, G., A., In Physical encyclopedia, Prokhorov, A., M.; Ed.; Bolshaya Rosiyskaya Entsiklopediya: Moscow, 1990, Vol. 2, pp 238–239.

Shoulders, K. Infinite Energy, 2005, 61.

Solin, M. I. Physical Thought in Russia; 2001, no.1, 43–58.

Spillane, S. M.; Kippenberg, T. J.; Vahala, K. J. Nature; 2002, 415, 621–623.

Storms, E. Tenth International Conference on Cold Fusion, USA, Massachusetts, Cambridge, August 2003.

Szpak, S;, Mosier-Boss, P. A., Dea, J., Gordon, F. Tenth International Conference on Cold Fusion, USA, Massachusetts, Cambridge, August, 2003.

Taleyarkhan, R. P. et al Journal of Power and Energy; 2004 218 (5), 345–364.

Torchigin V. P. On the nature of Ball Lightning, Doclady Physics vol. 48, no. 3 pp. 108-11 (2003).

Torchigin V. P., 2003 Optical Resonators in the Atmosphere. Laser Physics 13, no. 6, 919–931. 2003

Torchigin V. P., A. V. Torchigin, 2005 Physical Nature of Ball lightning. European physical Journal D 36, (2005), 319–327.

Torchigin V. P., Torchigin A. V., 2004 Role of Ball Lightnings in Low Energy Nuclear Reactions. Infinite Energy 54, (2004), 46–50

Torchigin V. P., Torchigin S. V., 2003 Optical solitons at propagation of whispering gallery waves. Quantum Electronics, 33 (10), (2003), 913–918.

Torchigin V. P., V.A. Suchugov, I.K. Krasuyk et al., 2003 Change in the wavelength of light radiation stored within an optical resonator by means of an acoustic pulse. Optics

Torchigin V. P.Acousto-optical devices USA patent number 6771412 of 3 August 2004.

Torchigin V.P. 2002. About stability of spherical layers of compressed air formed by intense light. Investigated in Russia. Electronic Journal. http://zhurnal.ape.relarn.ru/articles/2002/093.pdf (In Russian).

Torchigin V.P. Amplification of light in lightguides and resonators formed by acoustic wave. J. Tech. Phys. 66(8) 1996 107.

Torchigin V.P. Conversion of the light in a focon by the use of an acoustic wave as a pump. J. Tech. Phys. 66 (4), 128 (1996).

Torchigin V.P. Is it possible to consider the Ball lightning as a reason of the Chernobyl tragedy? Bulletin of Atomic Energy 84 89-92.

Torchigin V.P., A.V. Torchigin An increase in the wavelength of the light pulses propagating through a fiber. Physics Letters A, 311 (2003) 21.

Torchigin V.P., A.V. Torchigin On phenomenon of light radiation from miniature balls immersed in water, Physics Letters A 374 (2010) 588-591

Torchigin V.P., A.V. Torchigin, Features of Ball Lightning stability, Europhysics Journal D 2005, 32, 383–389.

Torchigin V.P., A.V. Torchigin, Phenomenon of ball Lightning and its outgrowth. Phys. Lett. A; 2005, 337, 112–120.

Torchigin V.P., Torchigin A.V. Behavior of self-confined layer of light radiation in the air atmosphere. Phys. Lett. A. 2004, 328/2–3, 189–195.

Torchigin, A.V. Torchigin Ball Lightning as an Optical Incoherent Space Spherical Soliton. In Handbook of Solitons: Research, Technology and Applications. Editors S.P. Lang and Salim H. Bedore. Novapublishers (2010) 3-54

Torchigin, A.V. Torchigin Chapter 6 Ball Lightning as an Optical Incoherent Space Spherical Soliton. In book Lightning: Properties, Formation and Types Editor Matthew D. Wood Novapublishers (2011) 133-184.

Torchigin, V. P. Lomonosov; 2003 no.2, 86-90.

Torchigin, V. P. Manifestation of Optical Quadratic Nonlinerity in Gas Mixtures. Physics; 2004, 49, No.10, 553–555

Torchigin, V. P., Torchigin A. V., Space soliton in gas mixtures. Opt. Comm. 2004 240/4-6, 449-455

Torchigin, V. P., Torchigin, A. V. Chemistry and life, 2003, № 1, 12–15.

Torchigin, V. P., Torchigin, A. V. Mechanism of the Appearance of Ball Lightning from Usual Lightning. Doclady Physics; 2004, 49, No. 9, 494–495

Torchigin, V. P., Torchigin, A. V. Propagation of self-confined Light radiation in Inhomogeneous Air. PhysicaScripta, 2003, 68, 388–393.

Torchigin, V. P., Torchigin, A. V. Self-organization of intense light within erosive gas discharge. Phys. Lett. A; 2007, 361, 167–172.

Urutskoev, L. I. Lomonosov; 2002, 10, 8-12 (In Russian).

Urutskoev, L. I., Fillipov D. N.. Usp. Fiz. Nauk; 2004, 174, № 12, 1355–1358.

Vihman E. Quantum Physics; McGraw-Hill Book Co.: 1967.

Vysotskii, V. I.; Shevelev, V.N.; Tashirev, A. B., Kornilova, A. A., Tenth International Conference on Cold Fusion, USA, Massachusetts, Cambridge, August, 2003.